# Praise For
# The Sage

"*The Sage* is Ron Bartalini's latest creation. I love this book. It is soothing and it brings peace to my soul." **Mark Lundskog, BS, CFO**

"The author of this book, Ron Bartalini, has drawn on his many life experiences, research, and introspection to enrich us with various literary offerings, including children's books, along with others for mature readers. This latest volume, '*The Sage*,' provides many insights and is a very worthwhile read." **William L. Baker, PhD, Higher Education Consultant**

"*The Sage* is an enjoyable, philosophical and spiritual epistle. The author, Ron Bartalini, steeped in a knowledge: of the scriptures and the saving doctrines of the gospel, has compiled an inspiring set of questions and answers that both illuminate and edify the soul of one searching for truth." **David Galbraith, PhD, Former Stake President, Former Mission President, Bulgaria, Sofia Mission**

"Regarding Ron Bartalini's, '*The Sage*,' What a beautifully written book of instruction, insight and inspiration." **Rose Mary Lindberg, MS**

# THE SAGE

## Ron Bartalini

Sundie Enterprises
Since 1972

ISBN 978-0-9991261-3-4
Library of Congress Control Number
2017913681
Bartalini, Ron

Cover art, Simeon and Jesus by
© Andrey Shishkin
(Free images of Simeon and Jesus).
Interior art, The Creation of Adam, by
Micelangelo Buonarroti
(from Wikipedia, the free encyclopedia).

## Description

God called his servant living on the earth to stand before his throne. God's servant was given the task of finding one certain young man who had lost his way. He was given the precise words to say to the young man. When the lost young man was found, the Lord's servant spoke the words given to him by God and the lost young man's heart was struck and he repented of his old ways.

He who was lost was told he must be baptized by one in authority and receive the gift of the Holy Ghost then continue to keep God's commandments and endure until the end. The young man became the first convert of God's messenger and he converted many others.

God summoned his servant yet again to stand before his throne. God praised his servant for his success. The Lord's messenger was then given the task to return again to the earth and take the gospel of Jesus Christ to the far corners of the earth. To baptize all believers, to give all these the gift of the Holy Ghost and to ordain those worthy with the authority to preach the gospel, to baptize, and to give the gift of the Holy Ghost to all those believers who are worthy to receive it and to call all the worthy to be missionaries throughout the world.

Published by Sundie Enterprises
P.O. Box 1274
Provo, Utah 84603-1274

# Contents

# *The Sage*

Ron Bartalini

# Dedication

To every nation, kindred, tongue and people living on earth.

# THE SAGE

## Prologue

There was a day when the God of heaven called his servant before his throne and said, "Go into the world and find that soul who has lost his way and say unto him, the God of heaven would bless your life with bounteous blessings but you are not ready to be blessed, you have not prepared your life to be blessed, therefore the blessings that would be yours must be given to another. When that man was found, the Lord's servant spoke those words to him in the light of day for he could not approach him in the night. And that young man knew in his heart that he had given his life to riotous living and that he had wasted the inheritance given unto him by his father and he was ashamed when thus confronted.

When he had first heard the words of God's servant, his heart was struck as if by lightning and it was as if an electric shock had pulsed

# THE SAGE

through his body. He was spiritually awakened on that day and he said to God's Servant, "What then must I do to be worthy to be blessed by the God of heaven and earth?" The Lord's messenger then spoke these words to the young man:

Your task is the same as it is for all those who have lost their way. You must acknowledge that you have sinned and come short of the glory of God. Then you must ask the God of heaven to help you change your life. Ask God to soften your heart that you might be able to repent of your old ways by confessing and forsaking your sins that you might be worthy of baptism that your sins may be washed away through the merits of the atonement of Jesus Christ. Covet baptism therefore, for baptism is the gate that all must pass through to find the kingdom of God.

When you have been baptized in the name of Jesus Christ: by one in authority you will then be prepared to receive the gift of the Holy Ghost. Let the Comforter, which is the Holy Ghost be your guide and companion throughout your life once you have received it. If you will do so and then continue to keep God's commandments and endure until the end, you will have joy in

# THE SAGE

this life and eternal life in the world to come. The young man did follow every word given to him by the Lord's servant and he became the first convert of God's messenger. In the days that followed the young man helped many to find God and follow the path that leads to eternal life.

God summoned his servant yet again to stand before his throne and the God of heaven praised his servant for his success.

Go now again to the earth and preach the gospel of repentance to all who will hear it. Give authority to baptize to all who are worthy to receive it. Call the pure in heart to be missionaries to go to the far corners of the earth to preach the gospel of Jesus Christ. Declare to the faithful that temples must be built upon the earth that the ordinances of the holy priesthood may be received by proxy by the living for those who are now dead and do now live in the world of spirits. Visit the believers who are faithful in many lands as well as those who have yet to hear the name of Jesus Christ. Teach the faithful and the non-believers that if they will repent and keep my statutes, they will be given power to

# THE SAGE

heal the sick and to cast out devils and even raise the dead according to their faith. Teach them that the Son of the living God even Jesus Christ is the Savior of the world and that He is their advocate with the Father. Testify to them that Jesus Christ is the only name given under heaven whereby men may be saved.

Organize the faithful to serve missions in every corner of the world. Tell the faithful that temples must dot the earth that the adversary may have his power abated for with every temple built and dedicated the power of the adversary is diminished. Take the gospel of Jesus Christ to the far corners of the earth for all must be able to hear it that they may choose for themselves before the Lord returns to the earth in glory.

You will be led by my Spirit not knowing where you should go yet my Spirit will guide your way. Seek out the pure in heart and call and ordain them to do even as you have been called to do. The Lord's servant thanked the God of heaven and spoke: All will be done according to thy bidding.

# CHAPTER ONE

## God's Servant
## Begins His Ministry

A wise man came into the village of many people long ago and stood before them and the elders of the village who were assembled, to hear him.

Speak the wisdom you have acquired from your many years of learning and experience and we will listen, and will hear, said he who was chief among those of the village.

The man stood still and remained silent for the space of half an hour and then he spoke: If you are not going to heaven by your works, you are going to hell by your works.

All the people of the village heard that saying of the wise man and as they were pondering those words in their hearts, a lonely figure appeared on the horizon. He was dressed in a white robe and he was carrying a staff. He approached the village slowly and when he finally stood before the elders of the village he spoke softly. What wisdom has the wise man

# THE SAGE

offered you on this day? The stranger spoke.

And he who was chief among those of the village answered him with the words of the wise man.

Not so, said the stranger. For if you spend the days of your probation on earth doing nothing; if you remain the same, you have sealed your fate, and condemned yourself.

The God of heaven and earth would have you get better every year. But to remain the same is like being stagnant water that becomes bitter then putrid.

"I perceive that thou art a man of God," said he who was chief among them. "Please impart to us the wisdom heaven would have us know."

The Lord's servant continued: Know ye not that God made man in his own image? Know ye not that God exists and God is real? Know ye not that the devil is real? Do you not know that Satan walks up and down the earth like a raging lion waiting to drag you down to hell and destroy your soul and sift you as wheat?

Choose ye this day whom; you will serve. This life is the time to choose. You have to make a decision. You must get better each year and not stay the same or get worse. If you stay the same, you seal to yourself the same fate as those who serve the devil.

# THE SAGE

Do you understand? And he who was chief among the elders said, "I do understand." If you understand, see that you change your life and begin to draw near unto God by loving God:
and keeping His commandments. If you do so, God will draw near unto you. Teach your people to do these things by your example, and all will be well with you and your people.

Is there yet more wisdom you would impart to us? The chief of the elders asked the man of God?

That is all you can bear at this time, said the Lord's servant.

And he turned and began to walk away slowly. When he reached the crest of the hill in the distance, he stood still as the sun went down around him and when the sun descended, he too, had vanished.

# CHAPTER TWO

## The Lord's Messenger
## Challenges This People
## to Repent

The morning sun was just edging its way up above the horizon as he approached the nearby city. He was walking across the plains of Gilead. Besides his robe, sandals and staff he carried nothing with him but the words God had put in his heart. An old man approached him as he entered the borders of the city. Sir, I perceive that thou art a messenger sent by God. What have you to say unto my people?

Go into the city and tell the people I will wait here and speak the words of God to them for three days that they might be able to repent and be saved in the kingdom of heaven.

The old man made haste to the heart of the city and noised about what he had been told. Many people followed the old man on the first day to listen to Lord's servant. The visiting stranger sat himself down on the crest of the hill when the people of the nearby village gathered to hear him. Then he began to speak to them in a soft but forceful voice:

Be it known unto you all that I am not the light and life of this world. I am but the voice of one crying in the wilderness sent to you to testify of that light. It is the light of Christ that lighteth every man that cometh into the world. He is the light that gives life itself to every living thing. Jesus of Nazareth is that light. He was born of Mary and walked among you but few came to know him. Yet he was the very Son of the living God, the creator of heaven and earth and your people caused him to be nailed to a cross on Calvary. Yet you could not take his life from him. He freely gave his life that all men might not have to suffer as he did if they would repent of their sins and acknowledge Him as the Son of God. If men will but believe that Jesus Christ is the Savior of the world and repent of their sins by their own choice, they may then be baptized in his holy name and have their sins washed away and receive the gift of the Holy Ghost. Then if they choose to endure until the end, the promise of the Father is, you shall inherit the kingdom of heaven unto eternal life.

You must make the choice to believe in Christ, to repent of your sins and to love God and keep his commandments. You and you alone must choose. No one can do that for you. When the day-of judgment comes you will stand before

# THE SAGE

God: to be judged alone. There will be no one else with you to hold your hand or to answer for your sins. You alone must answer for all you have done while you lived on the earth. Did you reach out your hands and your heart to help others while you lived your life or did you spend your allotted time thinking only of yourself and helping only yourself? How will you answer? Choose you this day whom; you will serve. Will it be God or will it be the enemy of all righteousness even Satan or the devil? You must choose. What will you do? Will you walk away? Will you hesitate? Will you procrastinate the day of your repentance until it is everlastingly too late? And at that moment some did walk away.

I will spend one more day with you to hear your answers. On the morning of the third day I will baptize all who choose to repent and then instruct you further. On the evening of the third day I must leave you. I have many others to preach to. There are many nations, and many people who have yet to even hear the name of the creator of all things, even Jesus the Christ. I am anxious to declare Christ unto them.

In the morning of the morrow even as the sun rises I will return to teach you. Return to your homes now and pray to the Father in all sincerity of heart. Speak to your heavenly

# THE SAGE

Father, even as the Savior of the world spoke to your fathers and taught them how to pray, do you likewise.

# CHAPTER THREE

## Of Prayer

ill you then teach us to pray? One man asked.

How easy it is for men to pray fervently to God when they are in need. God hears all such prayers and he will answer whom he will. But should a man pray to God when all is well with him and that man thanks the Father of us all for the very air he breathes, a roof over his head, a warm bed to sleep in, food enough to eat, good friends and family and for all unseen blessings and the beautiful world God has given him to live in, do not think that the heart of God is not touched by the prayer of such a man.

The best prayers come from the heart and not from the mind. A prayer is the song of the heart and not the thoughts of the mind. The best prayers therefore, come from the feelings of a grateful heart.

Before you pray, listen to the essence of whom God is, and you will hear his voice echoing through endless space speaking words of gratitude, thanksgiving and peace to your heart. Speak those words when you pray, and God will hear your prayer because you will be one with the thoughts of God. Remember, love is of God because God is love. There can be no bitterness of soul, no thoughts of rebellion or vengeance. No thoughts of animosity towards your neighbors because it is impossible to hate your neighbor and love God. Pray for the needs of others when you pray and let your thoughts of ministering to the needs of the poor, be lifted up into heaven as if on the wings of eagles.

ɧ  ɧ  ɧ

Let your heart feel the suffering of the less fortunate and you will understand how to pray. If all you do is pray for yourself, your praying is nigh unto vanity. Selfishness is not of God.

ɧ  ɧ  ɧ

God is not a man that he is selfish and cares only for himself. God is the author of love and all things unselfish. The Father gave his greatest treasure, his well beloved and only begotten Son as a sacrifice for all of his children that all might be saved if they would but believe and love the your prayers include chosen Savior and keep his commandments. Let your thanksgiving for this supernal gift of the Father to all of his children.

ᚠ    ᚠ    ᚠ

Who prays for the sparrow huddled together with his family on frozen branches facing a cold winter's day when the temperature drops below freezing? And if no one prays for the sparrow, who prays for the homeless man who wanders the city streets carrying all his possessions from one location to another until night falls and he must seek refuge in yet another strange place and still face another day not knowing if there will be food to eat as a new morning begins?

The Father of us all is aware of the sparrow and the homeless. It is man who has yet to understand whom it is he should pray for and it is seldom himself.

ᚠ    ᚠ    ᚠ

Now return to your own homes and pray. Pray into the night not one prayer but many. Speak to God that he might hear you. God will hear the sincere prayers of any of his children. For you are all sons and daughters of a loving Father in

# THE SAGE

heaven. I will return in the morning to answer your questions but now I must leave you.

The man of God walked away from those gathered at the crest of the hill. When he was but a stone's throw away, he vanished from their sight as if a portal had opened.

# CHAPTER FOUR

## Of Truth

**E**arly on the second day, just as the new sun was rising, the Lord's servant stood silently on the crest of the hill on the edge of the village. Many were already there waiting. Many others came to hear.

Speak to us of truth one man began.

Every man has his own version of truth within him and yet truth remains the same. Truth exists in and of itself. Truth was not invented or created by man. Truth has always existed as truth. Truth waits on man for its discovery. Many men believe the tradition of their fathers to be the truth but the traditions of men do not equal truth. All traditions should be tested and examined for the devil uses the traditions of men to deceive men and give all men a false sense of security.

Truth will pass any test and truth will not change as time passes. Truth stays the same throughout the ages. All truth leads men to light and more light. Light leads men to love. Love causes men to love their neighbor. Loving another leads men to God.

The "word of truth" or the "word of God" is found in the Holy Scriptures. The word of truth is hard for the unrighteous and rebellious to bear for truth condemns the sinner and does not justify him at all but requires him to repent. But for the righteous and those who love God, the words of truth are like pure spring water given to a man in the desert dying of thirst.

The word of God guides men to the light shining in the darkness. The light of Christ is pure truth and there is no confusion or darkness in it. Your truth is not necessarily another man's truth. Your opinion could also be your truth. But God's truth remains the only source of pure truth.

One of God's name titles is, "Truth." Truth is light. Truth is love. God possess all truth. God is not looking for new truths or more truth. That is one of man's occupations. God already holds all truth in the palms of his hands. When man comprehends "pure truth" man begins to comprehend God.

# CHAPTER FIVE

## Of the Creation of Man

peak to us now of the creation of man, if you please.

In the beginning of beginnings God was in his heaven. And God looked out upon the endless expanse of unorganized space filled with chaos and covered in darkness.

And God beheld the darkness and said, "Let there be light. And there was light." And God stood in the midst of all the billions upon billions of intelligences that were not created or made but have always existed. And God perceived that the intelligence he possessed was greater than all the other intelligences combined. And God deemed it wise and prudent to organize all the intelligences, which possessed the light of truth. God organized these as spirit personages after his own image and likeness. And it was so.

The firstborn spirit offspring of our Father was Jesus Christ, he who is and shall be the Savior of the world.

# THE SAGE

Although not the first spirit son of our Father, Adam was the first man to walk the earth, the first flesh also.

You are all sons and daughters of a loving Heavenly Father. You all lived with him in heaven before you came to this earth. All came to the earth to be tested to see if they could find and remember God and be willing of their own choice, to love God and keep his commandments.

And then the servant of God asked, Are there any sick among you? Bring them forth and I will heal them. And among those brought forth were the lame, the halt, the deaf, the dumb, the blind, and those who were suffering from all manner of diseases including the lepers. And when these were brought forth, the Lord's servant did heal them all.

Go back to your homes now and pray yet again that the God of heaven will soften your hearts that you might be able to feel his Holy Spirit touch your heart and soul. As the sun rises on the morrow, I will baptize all who are willing to confess that they have sinned and are willing to forsake their old ways and receive the saving ordinance of baptism for the remission of their sins.

And now I must ask you, do you understand what the Son of God has done for you because of his atoning sacrifice for you? Has that marvelous sacrifice sunk deep into your hearts? Do you feel the need to turn your life around or will you continue in your old ways? This is the time for you to repent. God has sent his messenger to you at this time. Will you procrastinate the day of your repentance or will you receive the pleasing word of God and be blessed? On the morrow you may be baptized and open the gate to eternal life. This is the way, the truth and the light. There is no other way.

On the morrow just as the morning sun was rising over the nearby mountains and casting its light and warmth on the people, the man of God returned. More than one thousand believer were baptized on that day. Those among them who were men, were ordained to the holy priesthood. These were given authority to baptize in the name of Jesus Christ, and they were also ordained to the higher priesthood and authorized to give the gift of the Holy Ghost to all who would receive baptism for the remission of sins. Many were called to be missionaries to go to the far reaches of the world to preach the gospel of Jesus Christ. Others were instructed to begin building a temple that those who had died could be baptized by proxy by the living for all must receive the ordinance of baptism to enter the kingdom of heaven, both the living and the dead.

# CHAPTER SIX

## Of Raising the King's Son
## from the Dead

hen the Lord's servant healed hundreds of the sick, lame, deaf, blind, and those who were lepers, the news of that event spread throughout the land and entered the ears of the king of a nearby kingdom. The king then sent messengers to summon the man of God to stand before him for his son was nigh unto death with a fever.

The servant of God did travel to the land where the king resided and ruled over a nation but by the time he arrived the king's son had died. The king was wrought with sadness nigh unto death. His grieving for his beloved son could not be abated. The Lord's servant stood before the king and said, Be of good cheer for your son will yet live. This thing is done for a witness of the power and glory of the Son of the living God that all might know for themselves that Jesus Christ is the resurrection and the life.

# THE SAGE

This is done that all may realize that Jesus Christ, has conquered death, by the power of the resurrection and because of the infinite atonement. Jesus Christ has atoned for the sins of all mankind and this has brought to pass the resurrection whereby all men may be lifted up at the last day. Fear not o king and grieve no more for the God of Israel shall work a mighty work before you that you might believe and testify to all your people of the reality of a living God.

I must prepare my own self with fasting and prayer for the space of one day and then I will return. Be of good cheer for the Lord has promised that your son shall yet live. I must depart to prepare myself to be receptive to the mercy and kindness of a loving God.

On the morning of the following day the man of God stood before the king once more. Take him to my son, the king commanded his servants. When the Lord's messenger stood before the king's son he laid his hands on his head and spoke, O God the Eternal Father, I know thou hast heard my prayer and I know that all power is in thy hands. In the name of Jesus Christ let the lad's spirit enter once again into his body and let the son beloved of his father yet live.

# THE SAGE

With that, the young lad rose up and his eyes fastened on his father, and the two embraced with the love only a father and son can share. The king's heart was filled with gratitude to the God of heaven for what had been done. And he said unto the Lord's messenger, tell me now what I should do to worship your God for truly your God is God and there can be no other.

On that day many of the subjects of the king came unto Christ and the man of God baptized them all and gave those who were pure in heart power to baptize and to heal the sick from all manner of sicknesses and every human malady, according to their faith.

Then the Lord's servant spoke to the king and said, call your people together that they might all be assembled before me. When the people were assembled before him he spoke these words:

Please know that I did not raise the king's son from the dead. It was the Lord God almighty that did this that you might believe in him and keep his commandments. I am but a servant of the most-high God. Let all the honor and glory be given to God and know this that if you will now love the God of heaven and earth and keep

# THE SAGE

his commandments and endure until the end, the Father of us all has promised you; you shall have eternal life.

And now that you have been converted what must you do? You must continue in the way. Moreover, all who have been converted are now responsible to strengthen and share their testimony of the gospel of Jesus Christ with the remainder of God's sons and daughters. For you are all the spirit sons and daughters of a loving Heavenly Father. Your Father wants all of his children to return to live with him in heaven. Your mission, if you choose to accept it, is to bring the gospel of Jesus Christ to all the ends of the earth. Therefore, all who now feel the Spirit of God weighing upon their heart to do this, arise and come forward and I will ordain you as ministers of Jesus Christ that you may be missionaries to all who have yet to hear his name.

Many hundreds then came forward and the Lord's minister gave them all the authority to preach the gospel of Jesus Christ and to baptize and to give the gift of the Holy Ghost.

The angels in heaven sang praises unto the God of heaven on that day and all the morning stars sang together.

# CHAPTER SEVEN

## Of Addressing
## His Fellow Travelers

On another day, God's servant entered a ship to catch the west wind that would carry him to a new land. While on his way, the people traveling on this sailing vessel approached him and bade him speak the words of God to them.

The Lord's messenger began by saying:

There are those who cannot speak without using profanity. Such are the simple minded and fools of the world. Do not listen to them for they will lead you to destruction, which is their end.

&#10013;   &#10013;   &#10013;

There are those who choose to use slang with each sentence they speak. These are they who wish to be accepted by others yet they do not choose to think before they speak.

# THE SAGE

There are those who use words to criticize others. They know what they are doing. They would have others think of them as superior but they should be pitied for their behavior marks them as being insecure and lacking in refinement.

ᚠ   ᚠ   ᚠ

God is not a personage who speaks as a man. God does not criticize man nor condemn man nor make idle threats. God lifts man and gently persuades man to look up and become even as he is.

ᚠ   ᚠ   ᚠ

Do you not know that words are powerful? When the creator of all things spoke, "Let there be light," the very elements obeyed him.

Should we not learn from this that words spoken with great faith have the power to influence the human heart? Let your words be spoken with happiness and the celebration of life and not a heavy heart. Let your words praise the creator of heaven and earth for the magnificent world he has given us to live in.

Let your words be filled with thankfulness and gratitude for all the seen and unseen blessings of life. Speak not words of sorrow but words of joy and happiness and joy will find you.

Let your words be filled with the hope for a better world. Speak words of thankfulness and appreciation for the good things of life that have found you and for the sorrows of life, speak words of acceptance. Be wise enough to know that for all of life's trials, God is ever near the man or woman who has a thankful heart.

ɟ  ɟ  ɟ

The most powerful words are not spoken that you might hear them by the hearing of the ear.
ear. With but few exceptions, the words of God are felt and not heard at all. Yet when man feels such words which penetrate through the ether of time and space, those words when uttered by man will be clothed in the finest silks of gold, purple and silver and will cause a chink in the armor of even the hardest heart.

# CHAPTER EIGHT

## Of the Beatitudes

hen his ship made landfall, he made his way to the nearest village where many people lived. There was one from the ship who asked to follow him. I would follow thee and be thy disciple if I may, for you have the words of life. You may follow me, but the words I have are not my own but they have been given to me by the Lord God Omnipotent and you will be his disciple and not mine. It will be He who has atoned for the sins of the world that you follow, as do I, for I am but his servant.

When he arrived at the village, the residents were waiting for him. They knew who he was and why he had come to them. When God's servant greeted them the people said, we have prayed you to us. Please speak the words, which the God of heaven has put in your heart and we will listen and we will hear.

# THE SAGE

These were pleasing words for the man of God to hear and he responded by telling the people of this land that he would articulate to those who had ears to hear what was required for this people to be blessed by God. God's servant sat down on top of a hill covered with new spring grass and began to speak:

I am not come to declare myself as the light and life of the world. I am but a servant whose privilege it is to declare the light to you. Ye are all children of the light.

ff    ff    ff

Ye are the love of this world. But just as a diamond must be cut and polished in order to bring forth light, so must you be cut and polished by your sorrows and suffering that your hearts might be made strong and be capable of receiving light.

ff    ff    ff

Blessed are the truly honest in heart, for they shall find peace in this life.

# THE SAGE

Blessed are the teachable, for they shall be instructed from on high.

ߠ  ߠ  ߠ

Blessed are the forgiving; for they shall be forgiven by our Father which is in heaven.

ߠ  ߠ  ߠ

Blessed are those whose hearts are broken and whose spirits are contrite, for they shall enter the kingdom of heaven.

ߠ  ߠ  ߠ

Blessed are those who feed and clothe the poor and care for the widows and fatherless
of this world, for your joy cometh in the giving of love.

ߠ  ߠ  ߠ

Blessed are those who seek after peace for they shall be called the children of light.

ߠ  ߠ  ߠ

Blessed are ye when your hands are clean and your hearts are pure for ye shall see God.

# THE SAGE

Blessed are ye when men shall mock you for your desire to live in the light, for so persecuted they many who were before you.

ቲ ቲ ቲ

Blessed are ye when men shall threaten your life and your family and throw you into prison for declaring to the world that there is a light shinning in the darkness. Rejoice and take heart for great shall be your reward in heaven.

ቲ ቲ ቲ

Blessed are the faithful for they shall receive blessings upon blessings but in the wisdom of God's timing and not their own.

ቲ ቲ ቲ

Blessed are those who love God and keep His commandments and endure unto the end for they shall inherit all the Father has.

ቲ ቲ ቲ

Blessed is he who stops to help a stranger on the street corner holding a sign asking for help; for that stranger is the symbol of the Lord himself beckoning to all to love his neighbor.

# THE SAGE

Yeah, blessed is he who helps a stranger but more blessed is he who helps his neighbor without first being asked; but because he perceives his neighbor is in need.

ᚠ ᚠ ᚠ

Blessed is he who helps the unwanted, the uncared for and the unloved, for he shall be held in the arms of angels even as Christ was comforted by angels when he suffered in the Garden of Gethsemane.

ᚠ ᚠ ᚠ

Blessed are the poor but only the poor who are also lowly of heart for they shall inherit the earth.

ᚠ ᚠ ᚠ

Blessed are all those who seek peace on earth for peace shall find them in the world to come.

ᚠ ᚠ ᚠ

Blessed are all those who hunger and thirst after righteousness for they shall be filled with the Holy Ghost and the Comforter shall bring peace to their souls.

# THE SAGE

Blessed are the pure in heart for they shall see the manifestations of heaven and even God shall reveal himself to them but in his time and in his wisdom.

ƀ ƀ ƀ

Blessed are the truly humble for they shall stand in the presence of God.

ƀ ƀ ƀ

Blessed are all they who suffer for their testimony of Jesus Christ for theirs is the kingdom of heaven.

# CHAPTER NINE

## Of Qualifying
## to Enter Heaven

One man sitting near the man of God raised his arm and asked, May I ask a question please?

Speak on, the servant of God said.

Will you tell us then, what one must do to enter heaven?

God's messenger continued: It is the basic nature of all men to worry first about themselves. All men are inherently selfish. But no selfish person will enter the kingdom of heaven. Therefore, let all men humble themselves before God and share all they have with those who are wanting. It is easy for the poor to hear: A rich man will hardly enter heaven unless he helps the poor. But if you are poor and help not the less fortunate with what little means you have, you shall not see the kingdom of God. You shall look up at the poor in heaven who were also poor in heart and they shall look down upon you as you suffer for your neglect of all the poor in this life.

# THE SAGE

Do you hold feelings of hatred and revenge for your neighbor in your heart? All such feelings come from below and from he who is the father of all lies. God did not say, Thou shalt hate thy neighbor; and seek revenge upon thy neighbor for every offense against you.

There are those among you who say, I own my houses and lands. But of a truth, man owns nothing. Men are but the caretakers of lands and houses in this life. God holds all things in the palms of his hands. God has given you the very air you breathe and all He asks in return is that you love Him and keep His commandments and endure until the end.

Every one who judges another should assess himself and be aware that each time you do so, that act is recorded in the Lamb's book of life by the angels who are silently note taking and with what judgment you judge, you shall be judged. Judging another without the inspiration of the Almighty is judging another by man's wisdom. Man's wisdom is not sufficient to hold the life of another in any man's hands.

Judges of the earth beware. For unless your judgment comes from the inspiration of the Almighty: your judgment is man's judgment. How many men sit in prisons today because of unrighteous judgment? How many men have been executed because of unrighteous judgment? How many have suffered because

# THE SAGE

someone with man's authority judged them wrongfully? Judges of the earth reconcile yourself to God and repent while there is still time. For with what judgment you have judged, it shall be meted out to you one hundred fold in the next life. This is the justice, judgment and equity of God.

But we need man's laws here on the earth, the judges of the earth say.

However, God made the earth.

But without the laws of man, there would be chaos on the earth, other men say.

Moreover, without God, there would be no earth and if you take God out of the equation, in time, all of civilization will cease to exist.

# CHAPTER TEN

## Of Forgiveness

peak to us now of forgiveness if you please, one in the audience spoke.

Forgiveness is like soft rain falling on a man traveling through a desert for days without water to drink. He who forgives others and asks God to forgive him for his mistakes is wise. God will forgive whom he will but for man it is required to forgive all.

But what of the man or woman who is a liar and an adulterer yet helps the poor and gives refuge to the homeless? This is why men are not able to judge the true hearts of other men. Man sees only that which is the outward appearance of man. With his ears, he hears of the acts of other men but God looks upon a man's heart.

Moreover, no man or woman is perfect. To become such is why we are here on the earth. It is not our job to judge other men or women but to forgive them all and ask God to forgive us, in-

# THE SAGE

asmuch as all men are sinners. When the sun rises, does it not shine on all? When the rain falls to give life to the earth, does it not fall on all? Even so should all men love one another and share the earth's bounty. Man's job is not to judge his fellow man but to forgive and to lift his brother up. Any weak minded and foolish person can find faults in another. However, he who looks for the good in others looks with the eye of God.

If you were to take the life of the son of a king, he will not forgive you though you petition him and beg his forgiveness both day and night for many days and lay a king's ransom at his feet. He will not forgive, but will seek you out and hunt you down to take your life.

But if you will come before the throne of the king of kings kneeling in prayer, though you offer no treasure or ransom of money but a broken heart and a contrite spirit; the king of heaven and earth will forgive you and he will remember your sins no more.

Do you understand the meaning of forgiveness? How easy it is for men to misunderstand this word. But ye must understand to enter heaven. You must first forgive all others their trespasses against you before your Father will forgive you for your trespasses. Please be certain you learn to forgive

# THE SAGE

in this life. This is the time for you to understand and to live that which you have learned. Do not take these words lightly. Put them into practice and all will be well with you. No man or woman can forgive another without his or her heart changing to a kind and loving heart. The light of the body is in the eye and the wealth of a soul is in the beauty of the heart.

ₜ ₜ ₜ

There are those who say in their heart, I will help those in need as long as it doesn't take any of my time and as long as I have money to give but I had better get something back for the money I give.

This sentiment is wrong. It is false. It is a lie. That would be like saying, a bee makes honey only to eat all the honey himself. No man knows what tomorrow will bring. All men should say in their heart, If God, be willing; and if I work hard, taking nothing for granted and acknowledging the hand of God in all things, God will eventually bring me success.

# THE SAGE

Do you understand the importance of being humble during the days of your probation upon the earth?

In that day when the Savior of the world returns to the earth to claim his own, the wicked and all the proud shall be burned as stubble. When the earth is cleansed, then shall the creator of heaven and earth descend from heaven in the clouds to claim his own. Do you not remember that Christ got down on his knees and washed the feet of his disciples? That act of humility was done as an example for all to know how to behave. Do you understand that it is not wise to speak of your own greatness and successes unless you also speak of your own weaknesses and failures? Yet to let another speak of your achievements is the way of the wise.

ƀ    ƀ    ƀ

Do you wish to influence others to do good works? The power of influence does not come by lording one's authority over another. In order to have great power to influence the lives of those who come unto the sound of one's voice, that person must be meek and lowly of heart. Such a man must follow, the promptings of hea-

# THE SAGE

ven. That person must be able to hear and act upon the inspiration of the Almighty. That person must love God and keep his command-ments. Then just as the rising sun melts the morning dew such an one will have great power to influence the lives of those who come under the sound of his voice and even the words that he may write will touch the understanding of the pure in heart and they will feel the powers of heaven influence them to do good and to love.

# Chapter Eleven

## Of the Secret to Life

As a new morning began, the servant of God entered a place on the edge of the sea. There were many people living in this city commerce. A young man approached him saying, I perceive thou art a servant of God, will you tell me the secret to life?

The Lord's servant began in a soft but powerful voice:

The secret to life is not that there is a God in heaven and that God has made man in his own image and likeness. That reality is left for man to discover for himself. The true secret to life is this: All of God's sons and daughters possess their own God given agency to choose for themselves. Without it, life would cease to exist. It is God who is perfect and without sin. It is not so with man, for all men have sinned and man is yet imperfect. Therefore, there must; needs be a Savior. Because of the fall of Adam, the Father chose his only begotten Son, even Jesus Christ to atone for the sins of all of mankind. Jesus Christ is the chosen Savior and redeemer of the world.

# THE SAGE

Jesus Christ is the only name given under heaven whereby men may be saved. Therefore, if man will only ask, he can know that there is a God and that God is always there for man to guide him back to heaven.

All that is required of man is to love God and keep his commandments. This brings us back to agency for all men must choose, for themselves. When a man draws near unto God; God will draw near unto man. But the part of the puzzle that most men do not understand is that man must take the first step. That is where agency comes into the picture, for God has placed the power to choose in the hearts of all men. No man can take that power from you. No man can force you to do his will and bidding unless you allow him. No man can force you to be angry. No one can cause you to be happy. People may help matters by the way they treat you, but you alone choose to be happy or sad. You alone choose to feel sorry for yourself and you alone choose to get up again and fight for what you believe in no matter how many times you are knocked down. No one can take your freedom from you unless you allow it to happen. All men are born to be free and to choose for themselves. The secret to life is that you have the power to control your own destiny.

Have you considered this, for a new way to think and live your life? Why not say in your

# THE SAGE

heart and therefore let your new thoughts be:

Whatever life throws at me, I will take it cheerfully because if I moan and groan about it, if I complain about it, even if I discuss it with others in a complaining way, those feelings will only grow and cause me more damage. But if I take whatever happens to me with a new attitude one that understands that all of this is a part of my reason for coming to the earth to live and be tested, that all of this is just a part of my personal test and that God would not give me any trial that I could not handle, so I will choose to take it cheerfully and with a sense of humor knowing that by my trials and suffering I will grow and gain experience, that will make all the difference! No longer will I feel sorry for myself. No longer will I feel unwanted and unloved. No longer will I complain. No longer will I tell all of my friends how hard life is for me. I will now understand that this is all just a part of life. I will begin to trust God with a new commitment of love and understanding. I will show God by my behavior that I do believe He knows what is best for me. I will even begin to invite the correction of others. I will begin to prove to God that I believe that he corrects those he loves for this is how a man grows in wisdom.

If you will begin to live this way, I promise you, your life will take on a new meaning and whatever happens to you will be easier to get through.

# CHAPTER TWELVE

## Of Love and Of God

From thence, the Lord's messenger traveled to Asia where he met a large congregation of believers. They invited him to address them within their place of worship.

It is pleasing to me that you have chosen to live the gospel of our Lord and Savior, Jesus Christ. I have been given many words to speak to you by and through the Spirit of the Lord. Please know that the words I will speak are not my own but have come down from heaven. Be it known to you all that God the Eternal Father loves you and is aware of each of you and knows your needs. He only asks that you pray to him in the name of Jesus Christ and ask that which you desire and he will answer you according to your faith in our Lord and Savior.

# THE SAGE

Please remember that all things under heaven begin and end because of one's faith in Jesus Christ. And now let me sing praises to that which is the essence of God:

Love is the catalyst of all things in the universe. Why is this so? The naïve and the foolish may inquire. It is because he who is the supreme architect and intelligence of the universe has done all things because of love. It because of the love the Father has for all his spirit sons and daughters that he has provided a Savior to atone for the sins of man that by and through the infinite atonement of Jesus Christ all may return to live with their Father in heaven once again.

ȸ ȸ ȸ

Love did not begin with man for God was before man. If you would learn how to love, imitate the love God has for all his children. If God did not love his sons and daughters he would have allowed them to remain in heaven as his spirit children with no chance of progressing. Therefore, without God's love for his children there would be no earth upon which the children of God could dwell. There would be no air to breathe, no water to drink, no food to eat. But all this is provided by a loving Father for all. God's love is not limited by his fear that there will not be enough for his children to eat or clothes enough to wear, neither houses enough to live in. God has conquered doubt and fear and how did he do this? The answer is, God's love is boundless therfore his creations fill the universe and stretch to eternity for God is love and God is endless and his love goes on forever, worlds without end.

The love the Father has, for all his hands have made, is so great that this is the name he is known by throughout all of creation. God is love and love is of God. If God did not love his children, he would cease to be God. If you do not understand the love of God you will never be able to find God. God will always be illusive to the man who hates his neighbor.

And now for that man who declares, I love God, but I hate my neighbor and for good reason, my neighbor is a scoundrel.

Did you make man that you understand the workings of the human heart? Did you stretch out the heavens and give order to the universe? Do the morning stars sing together to praise your goodness? Is it you, they sing praises to, or is it the God of glory? How can you dare profess your love of God when you have yet to appreciate and celebrate the finest workmanship of his hands, which is your neighbor? You are a hypocrite and you lack understanding if you do so.

But you say, my neighbor is a scoundrel. How could God expect me to love him?

Though he be the worst scoundrel, he is also a son of God and your neighbor is good for something. What could that possibly be you might ask? He is good at being a scoundrel. And have you considered that he may know no other way to live? Have you also considered that if your circumstances were the same as his, you might also now be a scoundrel? Accept your neighbor as he now is and love him as he is now. For you would no doubt, expect him to try and accept and love you if your walk in life was the same as his.

Concerning love and God, the Father of us all does not invite man to love him intermittently and when it is pleasing for man to do so. God would have his greatest creation which is man, love Him with all of himself. Please be certain to understand that the commandment does not invite man to simply love God, but more explicitly presents God's requirement for man to love his creator with all of his being. If you take the words as an invitation to love God just a little bit and when it is convenient for you to do so, you are missing the meaning of God's first great commandment.

ﬀ   ﬀ   ﬀ

Pure love between a man and a woman is a gift from God. For not everyone will experience such love in this live. A man should allow his beloved to have her own identity and to yet share their lives as one. A woman should allow the man she loves to continue as his own self and yet to move with him as one sharing all they have.

ﬀ   ﬀ   ﬀ

And yet the greatest gift of the human experience is when a man and a woman who have love for one another can feel and understand one of the wonders of life in the same moment. That is the very instant when time can stand still for them.

ﬀ   ﬀ   ﬀ

The greatest love any human being will ever feel will be a mother's love. There is one caveat to this truth, and that is when a man lays down his life for a friend. And yet there is no mother who truly loves her child who would not do likewise for her offspring. This is the gift of motherhood.

ƀ    ƀ    ƀ

Children are God's gift to the world and the way for all men and women to stay young at heart. When man learns to love the innocence and purity of a child, man has also learned to love God. Children are without guile and cannot lie. Children speak the truth. Children are filled with hope and wonder. They are able to remember living with God and they may be able to teach the grown-ups great lessons about the meaning of life from time to time. Stay close to little children because they are very close to God.

ƀ    ƀ    ƀ

Parents; love your children. Show them and tell them. Sons and daughters; love your parents while they are yet alive, not by your words alone but by your deeds. Speak the words: "I love you," often and fasten your eyes upon their eyes when you say it. For if you do not, when

# THE SAGE

they are taken from you, the dawn will not break from sunrise until sunset when you will wish you did.

**ff    ff    ff**

   Wives; love your husbands and husbands love your wives. Children; love your parents. Keep their commandments for they will bring safety and long life to your soul. Single men and women; find a puppy to love. Remember; no love given out is love lost, for love will find you once again whether in this life or in the life to come. Every act of kindness and love enlarges the heart of man and allows it to expand to hold even more love.

**ff    ff    ff**

   The love of the world is not the love of God. For God is not a part of the lusts of the world. The love of the world causes men to seek after material things but God does not love material things. That is one of man's preoccupations. Love not the world neither the things of the world for they are not of God. Rather, seek to find God and to love God and to keep his commandments. Depart from evil. That is wisdom. Fear God and keep his commandments.

# THE SAGE

That is how the knowledge of truth begins.

ff    ff    ff

The love of the world leads to greed, envy, selfishness, confusion, misunderstandings and strife. Love for the things of God brings peace. Not the peace that man understands, but the peace that comes from God, which brings confidence that God is ever with the pure in heart.

ff    ff    ff

If a man will love God and keep his commandments, he will not fear man, which causes trepidation. The man who fears God will acquire wisdom, which is one of God's greatest gifts to man.

# CHAPTER THIRTEEN

## Wisdom of the Ages

There are yet many things I have to say to you, the Lord's servant continued:

There is a difference between the laws of God and the laws of man. The laws of man end for a man when he dies but the laws of God go on forever. Consider the vast expanse of the universe. There is no space in which there is no law and there is no law in which there is no space. All of the creations of God in the heavens have been given a law by which they move in perfect harmony one with another otherwise the morning stars could not have sung together neither could the sons of God shouted for joy.

ff     ff     ff

All the planets, moons and stars orbit a star of a higher order and their orbits are fixed until they reach those heavenly bodies nigh unto God.

# THE SAGE

It is the God given right of all men to be free, to have freedom. However, to have freedom, men must first be taught true principles in order to govern themselves.

ʦ   ʦ   ʦ

Pure truth comes from God and not from man Therefore, unless a man walks with God he cannot correctly govern other men. Is there a man meek and humble who can be found to lead my people, saith the Lord of hosts? That man will speak to me, and hear my voice and do my bidding. Unless he who leads my people walks with God the people will stumble. Can you not now see that dictators are not of God but are evil? Slavery is not of God and is evil. No man or woman should be subject to the will of another man or woman. All men and women have a God given agency to choose for themselves. Should agency be taken away, all of creation would cease to exist.

ʦ   ʦ   ʦ

One of the biggest mistakes natural man makes is this: He thinks he should know the why, how and wherefore of everything before he believes. Man should not confuse his right to question everything with his mistaken need to understand everything. Pure truth will stand the test of any question. But to understand everything will not be accomplished in this life. That is one definition of God. That is, He who understands everything is God.

ƀ　ƀ　ƀ

In order to put faith and hope into practice one must believe without seeing and without understanding and without having all the answers, that is what faith is. If you already had all the answers and understood everything, there would be no need for faith or hope. There would be no need for this earth experience. Man is here on earth to be tested to see if he will live by faith, not to succumb because of misunderstandings.

ƀ　ƀ　ƀ

The moment you let thoughts of doubt enter your mind faith must depart from it. That is an unwritten law. For faith and doubt cannot exist in the mind of man at the same time.

# THE SAGE

The earth is alive. Many have always considered mother earth to be sacred. Of all the millions of worlds God has created, it is the earth that will become sanctified and holy, to become the celestial kingdom where God and his Christ shall dwell. In the days of Noah the earth was baptized with water. All of the wicked, were destroyed by the flood. When the Savior of the world returns to the earth triumphant in immortal glory, the earth will be cleansed yet again by fire and all the proud and the wicked shall become as stubble. The earth shall then be sanctified and prepared to receive her king.

ₕ ₕ ₕ


Let me sing now of wisdom. Can you understand it? Can you hold it in your hands? Can you attain it in this life? The wisdom that is from above is pure, it brings peace to the soul, it is easy to understand, it causes men to be kind to one another, to love God and seek out all things that would lead men to God.

ₕ ₕ ₕ

I have observed a thing as I walk through this life and it has come before my eyes again and again: It is the way you treat people that determines who you are.

Life is not about you alone, it is also about how you treat the people around you.

ₕ ₕ ₕ

The greatest gift a man can give is not money or the material things money can buy. The greatest gift a man can give is his time and his caring for others. Be a servant and minister unto my people, saith the Lord.

ₕ ₕ ₕ

One of the distinctions of being human is that human beings make mistakes. When children are young, little boys break things and little girls have their feelings hurt. If you will not allow people to make mistakes, you are not allowing them to be human.

ₕ ₕ ₕ

The time to find God is when you are alive and breathing and living on the earth. Perhaps I should say, the time *to remember God* is when you are alive and breathing and living on the earth for we all lived with God before we came to live on the earth.

# THE SAGE

And now for those who are having a difficult time finding God and loving him, consider this: If you will begin by loving all that God's hands have made, you will find God in short order and upon finding him, it will be easy for you to love the creator of all things. For in finding him, you will begin to understand that God loves you because he made you and because God is love.

# CHAPTER FOURTEEN

## The Lord's Servant
## Enters a Wicked City

There was a day when the Lord's messenger entered a city that was inhabited by the descendants of a people who were idolaters and were guilty of every sin of immorality.

The Lord's messenger asked the leader of that people to gather his citizens together that he might speak to them. The Lord's servant began by saying:

The God of heaven and earth has sent me to you to call you to repentance on this day. This city is the most corrupt of all I have visited during my days upon the earth. Your citizens are guilty of every sin of immorality and ungodliness. You are still practicing idolatry from the traditions of your fathers. Your hearts, are now hardened; as to the things of God. Unless you repent and bring the fruits of repentance before God this day and forsake your sins, there is little hope for you but to find eternal damnation in the world to come and utter destruction in this life for God has sent me to give you the space of two days time to repent or be destroyed. You have today and tomorrow to repent or be destroyed.

ft    ft    ft

Bring your people before me again tomorrow and I will preach the word of God to them that they may all have the opportunity to hear. On the morrow the Lord's servant did speak the words of God to all in attendance. They were once again told of their many sins and given the opportunity to change their ways and to repent.

The leader of this people then spoke to the Lord's messenger:

You have spoken hard words against us, even unto our damnation and utter destruction.

ft    ft    ft

The words I have spoken are words of truth and they are not my words but the whisperings of the Spirit of God unto your salvation and not to your destruction. If your heart condemns you because of the words I have spoken, it is because you know in your heart that you are guilty of every word spoken against you. The

# THE SAGE

righteous and the pure in heart fear not the truth when it is given to them by a messenger from the Most high. The righteous rejoice-and ask for, more truth.

ƀ  ƀ  ƀ

Ye are not of God but of the devil and you do serve him by your works and therefore, the things of God are an offense unto you.

Even so, if you will acknowledge your sins before your maker, who has atoned for the sins of the world, the same Savior of the world that your father's caused to be crucified; if you will believe in Christ and repent with all your heart, even so you can be forgiven because of the infinite atonement of Jesus Christ.

What say you? Will you confess that Jesus is the Christ? Will you repent of your evil ways? Will you take upon you the name of Christ and be baptized in his holy name for a remission of your sins or will you remain in your filthiness?

ƀ  ƀ  ƀ

And on that day some did depart from the evil they had done and the sinful ways they had lived in. These took upon themselves the name of Christ and were indeed, baptized. And they did leave that city with God's messenger.

The majority of that city nevertheless, did continue in their old ways and were content to serve the prince of this world who is Satan.
And not long after the Lord's messenger departed, that city was destroyed.

ɮ    ɮ    ɮ

There were twenty-two souls both men and women who left that wicked city and walked with God's servant on that day. "Let us follow you to the four corners of the earth and preach the gospel to God's children from henceforth," they all said in unison. The Lord's minister gave them authority to preach the gospel then, and sent them out two by two to their separate places of the world to preach the gospel of Jesus Christ on that day.

Then the Lord's servant said, Depart in peace. May the Spirit of the Lord Omnipotent be with you always to guide, your way. Follow his Holy Spirit and be still and listen, for the whisperings of the Spirit of the Lord to your hearts and ye will know what to say and do. And may the Lord of hosts keep and protect you today and always until we meet again.

And now I must leave you, I have many others to preach the gospel of Jesus Christ to.

# THE SAGE

He turned into the setting sun then and when he was about 100 yards from them, he vanished before their eyes.

# Chapter Fifteen

## The Lord's Servant Returns During the New Millennium

Many days passed since God's servant had appeared and taught the people on earth the words he had been given of God. And the days passed until they became hundreds of years as measured by man. Then one autumn day, the man of God did appear to a small group of believers in a secluded place in a valley surrounded by mountains, far from the crowded cities of man. These believers lived in America in the time of the new millennium, a time when many of God's sons and daughters had lost their way because of the lies and deceptions of man.

The Lord's servant approached the people who were gathered outside of their place of worship. Wearing nothing but a white robe, sandals and having only the words, which God had given him to speak, the lord's messenger approached the group of about forty.

# THE SAGE

Greetings to all:

Thank you for living your lives as examples of the words of our Lord and Savior, Jesus Christ. Please know that I have been sent to you because of the way you have each lived your lives. It is because you have not just given lip service to the merits of the goodness of Christ but because you do serve and minister to the needs of each other that I have been permitted to visit you. Each one of your small acts of kindness; has been recorded by the angels in heaven and there have been many. Please know that I am but a servant of the most-high God and that the message I have been given to share with you comes from the Lord of hosts because of your faithfulness.

The people invited God's servant to sit on the green grass nearby where they could all also sit and gather around him. When he was seated he began to address them:

Should the leader of a nation who is caught in a lie be permitted to continue ruling that nation? For those who have ears to hear and eyes to see, please use your God given senses to hear and see and understand now. He who lies to those he has been elected to serve, is not of God, he is of the devil. God cannot lie or deceive. God knows that should he do so, he would cease to be God. Lucifer who became Satan or the devil

is the author and father of all lies. That is who
the devil is. He is a liar and as our beloved
Savior has said, he was a murderer from the
beginning. Those who lie will continue to lie because they are not of the truth.

☩    ☩    ☩

I have seen one thing in my days under the
sun that has not changed:
What a man does once, he will do again. And
what a man does to one, he will do unto
another.

☩    ☩    ☩

Should one who leads a nation do so by his
counsel or by the counsel of other men and
women? The wisdom that comes from above is
clear:
When the leaders of nations do not seek the
counsel of God, it will not be many days until
the people perish.

☩    ☩    ☩

There is one thing that will save all men and
redeem them from all sin even those who lie to

# THE SAGE

those they were elected to serve. If a man will acknowledge that he has sinned, then call upon God to help him repent by confessing and forsaking his sins; that man can be forgiven because of the infinite atonement of Jesus Christ. Christ came not into the world to condemn the world but to free the world from sin.

ꝶ    ꝶ    ꝶ

This is the pattern that has not changed since the first man Adam, was on the earth:

All men must acknowledge that they have sinned and fallen short of the glory of God. Then all must confess and forsake their sins. Then cometh baptism: for the remission of sins, by one in authority. To be properly baptized, one must be immersed under the waters of baptism, which symbolizes a washing away of past sins and a re-birth or being born again. Then that person can receive the gift of the Holy Ghost and the promise of the Father is, if you will endure until the end, ye shall have life eternal.

# THE SAGE

There are some who believe that everything they hear or read is the truth. If the people hear the same lie often enough, they will begin to believe it is the truth. But all things that portend to be truth must be tested. Does that which is purported to be the truth enlighten the mind? Does it cause one to believe in Christ and desire to do good works? Does that which is peddled as truth cause confusion? Does it cause contention and distrust and resentment and anger? These things lead men away from God.

ft    ft    ft

Satan is the author of all things that lead men away from God. The things of God are first pure then peaceful, filled with mercy and compassion and will cause the hearer of that light and truth to do kind acts and seek God out. That which causes contention, confusion, resentment and anger comes from below and is of the devil. All lies are of the devil for he is the author of all lies. All lies originated with Lucifer in the pre-existence and not with any man who has ever lived on the earth from the first man Adam, until today.

# Chapter Sixteen

## Comparing the Creation
## to an Automobile

peak to us now concerning the mysteries of creation with simple words so that we might understand.

The Lord's messenger then said, I will liken creation to an automobile:

The engine is the power of the car.

The holy priesthood after the order of the Son of God is the power of creation.

ff ff ff

The key to the car starts the engine.

The keys of the holy priesthood start priesthood power. For example, the key to creation is needed. The key to controlling the elements and walking on water is needed.

ff ff ff

The starter motor of the car allows the car to start. Faith allows all spiritual things to begin.

# THE SAGE

Without faith the sun would not rise each morning. Faith causes action.

ff    ff    ff

The battery of the car stores energy and also allows the car to start.

The temple is the place where we go to recharge our spiritual batteries. The ordinances of the holy priesthood are found inside of the Lord's temples. Temples are, the House of the Lord. They not only recharge our spiritual batteries by and through the spirit of the Lord which rests therein they also allow us to understand the mysteries of God by and through the ordinances of the priesthood which are found there in rich abundance.

ff    ff    ff

The wheels and tires of a car allow it to keep moving down the road.

Prayer keeps us moving down the road of life. The Savior has given man, (words of power and faith in God, in his model prayer), For thine is the kingdom and the power and the glory forever, Amen. God spoke (words of power and faith) to the elements, Let there be light, and there was light.

# THE SAGE

The steering wheel of a car keeps the car on course.

Obedience to the commandments of God keeps man on course. God gave a steering wheel to the universe. To every space there is a kingdom and every kingdom has its law given. There is no space without a kingdom and no kingdom without space and to all these there are laws and bounds for the order and orbits of all the stars and galaxies.

 

    ff    ff    ff

The gasoline or other fuel source of a car allows the car to go.

Man's fuel or the thing that keeps man going is his hope for a better world.

God's fuel is his hope that all of his spirit sons and daughters will return to live with him again. That is his business model. That is his work order. This is his modus operandi: To bring all of his spirit children back to heaven, to enjoy eternal life with him.

    ff    ff    ff

The headlights of the automobile allow man to see through the darkness of the highways of life.

Christ Jesus is the light shinning in the

# THE SAGE

darkness of life itself and yet the darkness does not comprehend the light of the world.

A portion of the light of Christ has been given to every man that he might know the difference between good and evil. Moreover, it is the light of Christ that gives light to the moon, and the stars and the earth upon which you stand. The light of Christ is the power by which the sun gives her light. The light of Christ gives life to all things for without it nothing could live.

ɮ     ɮ     ɮ

There is therefore, darkness and there is light and we know from whence the light cometh. For he who is the light and life of the world, said to the darkness, Let there be light, and there was light.

ɮ     ɮ     ɮ

Agency can be likened to the nuts and bolts that hold the steering assembly of a car in place.

Without agency God's plan of salvation will not steer. In fact, without agency all of creation would cease to exist. God will force no man to heaven. Man gets to decide to choose the evil or the good.

# CHAPTER SEVENTEEN

## The Most Important Thing
## in Life

The messenger of God stopped to take nourishment by a well. A young man approached him with the look of deep concern in his eyes. I can tell that you are a man of God, the young man declared.

Will you tell me please, what is the most important thing in life?

The man of God began:

There are some who say, nothing is more important than money. Others believe fame, is the thing. For when you have enough fame, they say, money will follow. Still others insist nothing is better to have than power for if you can acquire it, you can have money and fame as well.

ft        ft        ft

What then is the truth of these things?

# THE SAGE

Money stays behind when you die and it will end up in the hands of another.

ft  ft  ft

Fame, if you find it can also slip through your fingers in one minute. The attention span of one's fans and admiring public can change without warning. So fame certainly is not the most important thing for one to acquire in this life.

ft  ft  ft

What then of power?

There have been many kings, dictators, presidents and rulers throughout history but few indeed, are remembered throughout the annals of time. Those who remain in man's memory do so, because they have done some good to help promote the welfare of mankind. Not forgotten are also those who have done something so evil that they are remembered for a time but most people who acquire power in this life are all but forgotten with the passage of time.

What then does matter? What should one spend his time doing as he walks among men in this life?

# THE SAGE

Here is wisdom: Find God. Come to know God by loving him and keeping His commandments. Fear God and depart from evil.

✝   ✝   ✝

This is the way to eternal life. There is life beyond the grave and you can take that sure knowledge with you when you die. Moreover, if you will choose to keep God's commandments by deciding to repent of your sins, be baptized by one in authority for the remission of sins and then receive the Holy Ghost, and endure until the end, the promise is, you will have eternal life.

✝   ✝   ✝

Money, fame, and power over others will vanish when you die, but the humble and meek of the world who care for the poor and less fortunate will find hope in this life and eternal peace in the world to come.

# Chapter Eighteen

## Of Tithes and Offerings

O n a certain day, the man of God stopped to visit a man who had been promising God in his prayers for seven years that he would eventually get around to paying his tithes and offerings. The Lord's servant had been instructed to search this man out and visit him. When he was found, the servant of the Lord began by saying:

I have been sent to you: by the Father of us all. He has listened to your prayers for seven years but you have yet to fulfill your promise of paying your tithes and offerings. You have been blessed with many material things and yet you cling to them even as steel holds to a magnet.

ẞ ẞ ẞ

How long will you continue to test the patience of God? Know ye not that God can take you at any time? Yet God waits on you for if he took you at this time you would not be prepared to receive all the blessings, which could be yours. But he has waited upon you to fulfill the promise of your prayers to pay your tithes and offerings.

ﬀ   ﬀ   ﬀ

Perhaps you believe secretly in your heart of hearts that your possessions are your own? You may surmise that your house, car, savings and all other material things are owned by you. To so believe shows a shallow faith and a lack of understanding. God holds all things in his hands. You are but the caretaker of all you possess while you walk the earth. Seven winters have passed and you have stayed the same. And yet the trees of the forest renew themselves each season by casting forth their seeds into the earth and when the next season begins do they not show forth, new growth?

ﬀ   ﬀ   ﬀ

Where is your growth? Where is your improvement? Cease to rob God. And do you suppose that God needs your money? It is you who needs God. For by giving that which you have, you too will be blessed with new growth.

# CHAPTER NINETEEN

## Of Temple Service

On a day when many of the faithful had come to serve in the temple, the servant of God addressed them.

Greetings: to all who have come to serve, the Lord. I too, am but a servant of the Most High God sent to you because of your good works. May the God of heaven ever bless you for your faithfulness and willingness to serve our beloved Savior, even Jesus Christ.

Please continue to do so, for when you enter the temples of the Lord the adversary has his power diminished. And each time a new temple is constructed and dedicated, the powers of the adversary are abated. Please know that the spirit of Elijah is real and powerful. Let the hearts of every son and daughter be drawn to the fathers and the hearts of every father be drawn back to their children. The living cannot enter heaven without the blessings of those who have died and entered the world of spirits; neither can the dead be redeemed without the saving ordinances of the holy priesthood.

# THE SAGE

I have just returned from the world of spirits where those men and women who have died and left the earth dwell. They cannot progress without the glorious work you do here in the temple. The ordinances of the Holy priesthood performed by you in the temples of the Lord in their behalf; are saving ordinances. Without them they cannot be saved and continue to progress but neither can you. The intention of our Lord and Savior is that all of mankind work together to be able to return to live with the Father of us all.

ﬀ    ﬀ    ﬀ

Understand that the spirit of man does not die and the men and women who live in the spirit world are not dead, they are living men and women who are very much aware of you. Those who are worthy can indeed look upon you and see the good work you do in their behalf.

When the day arrives that your physical self dies and your spirit leaves this earth and passes beyond the veil and into the world of spirits, the spirits of those you have performed the holy ordinances for in their behalf will kiss your necks and bathe your feet with their tears of gratitude and joy.

# THE SAGE

The work that you do here in the Lord's holy temples is vital to the fulfilling of the Father's plan of salvation. It is the desire of the Father that the family of man be welded together: from Father Adam who is the first man, continuing until the last family born. Every family must be sealed together, forever but they cannot without your help. Do you understand?

And those in attendance said, yes, we do understand.

ʄ ʄ ʄ

Then continue to continue, the Lord's servant declared. And you will receive blessings upon blessings and the angels of heaven will record your names in the Lamb's book of life.

ʄ ʄ ʄ

I give you a final warning: Beware of false Christ's and false prophets. They shall come as a lamb in sheep's clothing and will deceive many. Already, they have come into the world. Beware of false news from those who would deceive and confuse you to accomplish their own agendas. Be cautious and be discerning.

# THE SAGE

I would now speak to you of those who preach the gospel to get gain. Such are not of God but are led away by the lusts of their hearts. The lusts of the world are not of God but cometh of evil and from below. Love not the world neither the things that are in the world. Spend your time of probation on the earth by reaching out to the poor and by caring for, serving and ministering to the needs of your neighbor.

✠ ✠ ✠

Remember, it is a good thing to give to those in need when you are asked, but it is far better to give without first being asked because you see thy brother is in need.

✠ ✠ ✠

And now to all the faithful who serve in the holy temples of the Lord, to those who perform the saving ordinances for the dead by proxy, you shall be caught up in the morning of the first resurrection to meet the Savior when he returns to the earth in glory to gather his own.

# CHAPTER TWENTY

## Of Music

To yet another group of people living in the new millennium the servant of God appeared, to speak the words heaven had given him. These also recognized him as God's messenger sent to enlighten their minds. When all were gathered together, he who was their visitor spoke:

Music is the language of heaven but not the only one for God speaks every language that exists. Music adds a new dimension to mere words. When words spoken or written fail to touch the soul of man, music will soothe a restless heart and cause it to stir even as the spring breeze causes a songbird to sing and spring grass to flutter. Music awakens the immortal memories of man and enables him to remember walking with his heavenly king.

# THE SAGE

Music is the gift of God to man. A well written song is man's gift to God. Music is mathematically perfect. From the black and white keys of the piano man can write a million, million melodies. For he who has been blessed with the gift of song, nothing is more pleasing than the song whose lyrics and melody melt together as one.

ff   ff   ff

Music is how the heavenly hosts worship God. Music can touch the soul of man in ways that the language of words cannot. Singing praises unto God as man worships the Lord on the Sabbath day invites the angels to also attend. The prayers offered as man worships on the Sabbath day invites the Father to listen in. Music can quiet the soul and calm the troubled mind. The countenance of man smiles when his spirit hears the song of the heart.

ff   ff   ff

Music can do more to calm the troubled heart than many words found in a library of books. Music communicates to the spirit of man because music is a spiritual thing. The things of

# THE SAGE

God must be understood by the Spirit of the Lord; communicating to man's spirit. Music can greatly assist in this process.

ᚠ ᚠ ᚠ

The ability of man to think wondrous and supernal thoughts regarding the majesty of life and creation is but one of God's gifts to man. Conversely, the habit of thinking low and debasing thoughts will eventually be his undo-ing and ruin, for every choice of man has its consequences.

# CHAPTER TWENTY-ONE

## Of Death

efore you leave us will you speak to us of death? Will you assure our hearts that we will yet come to live with God? One man asked and his words were the prayer of his heart.

The Lord's servant looked upon that man with compassion, in his eyes and spoke these words:

There are some who say, when a man dies all is lost for his life ends forever. Nothing that God's hands have made ends but all of his creations go on forever. If a tiny acorn from the giant oak tree falls to the ground, does the oak tree die? In the glory days of autumn do the crimson leaves in the canyons not sing the praises of their maker? Though they fall to the ground and die, autumn leaves celebrate their days of living in brilliant colors with their song of life. Does not this tell us that death is a celebration of the days of life? Life continues and does not end. Neither should one's passing have to be thought of in sorrow. Mourning for those we have lost is good but it should not go on forever. Instead, let us thank God for the time we had with those we loved and submit them unto God who will care for our loved ones with a Father's love.

ff    ff    ff

God did not make man in his own image and likeness and breathe the breath of life into man's nostrils to have man's life end when he dies. Moreover, God has prepared a place for the spirit of man to journey to when his physical body dies. All things; have been prepared for man by a loving God. When the Son of man returns to the earth in a resurrected body clothed in glory, the righteous who are living shall be lifted up into heaven in resurrected bodies of flesh and bones. The graves will be opened and all the righteous who have slept; shall be lifted up to meet the King of glory.

# CHAPTER TWENTY-TWO

## Of Gaining Wisdom
## More Swiftly

A man who was a university professor asked:

Is there a way to speed up the process of gaining wisdom?

The Lord's servant answered:

If you will learn to ask clear, concise and intelligent questions when you speak to God, you will eventually realize that in so doing you already have half of your answer.

# CHAPTER TWENTY-THREE

## Of Knowing the True Heart of A Man

Is there a way to know the true heart of a man? A philosopher asked.

The Lord's servant then spoke:

No man can know another man's thoughts. This disclosure; is protected by God. However, the following will reveal much of the true measure of a man's heart:

Consider not so much the words a man speaks but that which he does. It is better for a man to serve God humbly by serving God's children than it is for a man to stand before men and tell them all the good he will do or all the good he has done. Keep silent about the good you do. Let others speak of your kind acts.

# THE SAGE

The man or woman who constantly speaks of themselves by repeating all of the times and places they served others, all of the positions of authority they held, and all of the good they have done is not the man or woman who will be spoken of by the angels of heaven and why?
The angels will not have anything left to speak of if those who do kind acts constantly speak of their own good deeds. Be a servant to God's children and keep silent. Minister to the needs of your family, neighbors, and friends and then keep silent. Lift up the hearts of the poor, and downtrodden; the widows and fatherless, the homeless and forgotten and then keep silent.

ﬅ    ﬅ    ﬅ

Consider asking yet other questions of yourself concerning anyone who's heart you would like to know: Does this person acknowledge that Jesus is the Christ? Does this person stand and say, Jesus has come in flesh to the earth? Doe he declare that Christ has suffered and died and has given himself a ransom to atone for the sins of the world? Does he give his witness that Jesus Christ is the only name given under heaven whereby mankind may be saved? Does he acknowledge that Christ has conquered death and that he has risen from the grave and now

# THE SAGE

lives in a resurrected and perfected body of flesh and bones? Does he bear witness that Jesus Christ is the Son of the living God and that he is the promised Savior of the world? Does he further, declare to all that Christ will return to the earth in glory to claim his own? Does this man or woman confess that they have sinned and they rely upon the merits of the atonement of Jesus Christ and the grace of Christ to be saved?

&#10013; &#10013; &#10013;

Conversely, does this person declare that he will be his own Savior and that he does not need Christ in his life? Does the person in question deny the existence of God and profess that the universe made itself and that all of creation did also? Does he or she further insist that money; material things, fame and power are all that matters in this life?

# CHAPTER TWENTY-FOUR

## Of Finding Favor with God
## and Man

Then a young mother with her two children close by her, asked:

Is there a way for man to find favor with both God and man?

The servant of the God of heaven then spoke:

Put God first in all things and give all the honor and glory to God. Be forgiving of others and ask God to forgive you. Be ever thankful and grateful to God for the blessings of heaven.

ⴲ　ⴲ　ⴲ

Concerning man: Never speak of the good you do. Let another speak of your kind acts of service. Speak only of the good works and kind acts of others. Never criticize or find faults with others. Celebrate the victories of others and encourage them to continue to reach for success. Never complain when you speak but

# THE SAGE

let your words be a celebration of life. Be positive and find grace even when the tests of life cause you the most sorrow and pain. Smile, say hello to those you meet. Shake their hands firmly; look into their eyes and say, It is good to meet you. Learn people's names and use their name each time you see them. Learn to employ the words, "please" and "thank you," often, in almost every sentence. Thank everyone for the opportunity and privilege to serve them. Be grateful and express your thankfulness and gratitude often. Let people feel of your warmth and concern and caring for them.

Doing these things will place you in good stead with God and man.

# CHAPTER TWENTY-FIVE

## Of Motherhood
## and Sacrifice

The Lord's servant came upon a group of believers, both men and women, who were working in the fields harvesting wheat. They had stopped to take their lunch on a table left out in the fields. They too, recognized this traveling visitor as a man of God. They invited him to take nourishment and drink with them and when that was done they asked if he would instruct them in the ways of God.

The Lord's messenger began:

Have you considered that which God has put into the heart of woman teaches us all to sacrifice? Motherhood is the supernal gift from God to woman, which includes the supreme duty of woman to bear the souls of man and instruct them so perfectly in the ways of God that they might be worthy to return to live with Him in heaven once again. This is an almost unimaginable trust by the creator of all things.

# THE SAGE

Mothers all over the world teach us that without sacrifice there are no blessings. But with sacrifice, the very windows of heaven open to shower God's blessings upon us. Mothers teach us that serving, ministering to, and caring for another allows us to love.

       ᚪ     ᚪ     ᚪ

Should you determine to serve others with an open heart and by performing many small acts of kindness it will be impossible for you not to come to love those you have sacrificed for after the passing of many days.

       ᚪ     ᚪ     ᚪ

What has been your sacrifice? What have you done without? You have not sacrificed unless that which you have given up causes you to hurt. Some may say; I gave my old coat to a poor man. But the Son of man had no coat to give and yet he gave his life that all might live. Another may say; I let a stranger sleep in my barn. But the Son of God was born in a manger because there was not room enough in the inn. Could you not let a stranger sleep in a warm bed for even one night?

# THE SAGE

Another may say; I let many strangers eat the leftovers from our thanksgiving feast. Could you not invite them to dine with you and share your bounty when it was first served still fresh and warm? Still another may say, I did invite the poor into my home and let them sup with me and then I did clothe the naked with new raiment and then I did provide work and shelter for the poor. Which of these has made his sacrifice with an understanding heart?

ff    ff    ff

God would have you sacrifice for the poor by getting up close to them that you might feel their neglect. You cannot truly sacrifice for another at a distance. Should you do so, you will receive blessings from a distance without those blessings from God being close and personal. If you decide to do a kind act for another, do it with all your heart and God will bless you with all of his heart.

ff    ff    ff

When you sacrifice for another get up close to them. Fix your gaze upon them that you might feel their pain, sorrow and suffering. When you

# THE SAGE

can see God's image in their eyes looking back at you, you will know that God accepts your sacrifice.

ɮ   ɮ   ɮ

Can you not see that it is the sacrifices we make for others by doing without ourselves and forgoing our own needs and pleasures that another soul might live in comfort for at least a day that raises us up high enough to sing with the angels?

# Chapter Twenty-Six

## The Importance of Families

ives follow your husbands in righteousness for this is the way of heaven. Fathers and mothers council with one another and allow each to speak their feelings on the matters at hand. When the moment presents itself and you will know when that is, you may wish to let your children instruct you for young children are very close to heaven and remember living with their Heavenly Father.

ƀ    ƀ    ƀ

It is the desire of your Heavenly king that families be sealed together through the eternities from father Adam until this present time. Families should stay together and they may if they are willing to keep God's commandments.

Know you not that you are a part of the family of God? God is your father and he knows you. God knows your very heart. You cannot hide from God although many men have tried and many more deny that God exists. God's eyes comprehend all that his hands have made.

ℜ   ℜ   ℜ

Look up into the heavens on a dark night far away from the lights of man and behold the creations of God.

Can you say; the heavens made themselves? Can you continue to believe that you can hide, from God? Every act of kindness man performs is recorded by the angels in heaven. Every transgression man commits, is seen by God and shall be noised about on the last day unless a man repents and then God has said, I will remember your sins no more.

ℜ   ℜ   ℜ

Why does God tell us that the lost sheep is so important to the shepherd? It is because the lost sheep represents one of God's children; who has lost his way.

ℜ   ℜ   ℜ

Fathers gather your children in your arms then look into each one's eyes and tell them that you love them and will always love them no matter

# THE SAGE

what mistakes they make. Spend your life teaching them to keep the commandments of God but not with your words alone: but by the silent sermon of your example.

&#10014; &#10014; &#10014;

To be a father is to be as God for that is the name He would be called by regardless of all the other names men pronounce upon him. Fathers teach your children to fear God and to depart from evil for this is the beginning of knowledge and understanding. Do not withhold correction from your children but instruct them to seek correction for when correction comes it will be because God loves them and you too, are but God's servant and messenger.

# CHAPTER TWENTY-SEVEN

God's Servant Testifies of Christ,
Gives Final Words of Wisdom,
and Bids All Who Love God, adieu.

nd now to all the ends of the earth, I remind you all that I am but a servant of the most-high God. I am but God's messenger crying in the wilderness, declaring to you that Jesus Christ is the light and life of the world. Christ did come to the earth in the flesh and he did walk among man in the meridian of time. He was the promised Messiah and he is the king of kings sent by the Father to redeem the world from sin. He was not known of his own people although some did recognize him through the Spirit of God and by the grace of God. The majority of all those whom he walked among rejected him as the Son of the living God and they did indeed eventually cause him to be crucified. Yet they could not take his life from him. He was given power from the Father to freely lay down his life to atone for the sins of all mankind and to take his life up again.

# THE SAGE

He came into the world to save the world from sin by laying down his own precious life for the sins of the world. He is the Savior of the world. He created the heavens and the earth and all things that in them are yet he walked humbly among man. He owned no great mansion. He possessed only a robe and sandals and made his bed on the desert floor or in the home of friends and strangers.

Few indeed, knew who he was, yet he knew all men and women and spent his days serving man and ministering to the needs of strangers, healing the sick, giving hope to the hopeless and casting out devils and declaring to the world that he was the Son of the living God sent to lift man up by laying down his sinless life that he might draw all men to him.

ɞ     ɞ     ɞ

And now to all the family of man I do declare that Jesus Christ is the promised Savior and there is no other. His name is the only name given under heaven whereby men may be saved. And thus it is, and forever will be. Amen.

These words and thoughts are for all men, both the believer and the non-believer:

# THE SAGE

A loving heart is a cheerful and a thankful heart. All of the angels in heaven smile, when one of the sons and daughters of God gives thanks unto God. It is easy to give thanks unto God when one understands where all good and blessings come from.

ft ft ft

When a man loves God he will keep God's commandments and the God of heaven will guide that man's steps. There are no coincidences under heaven for such a man. All that happens to him will be for his good.

ft ft ft

A misshapen heart and a misshapen mind are one in the same; they both lead to nonsense and confusion.

ft ft ft

There is one who is the author of confusion. He is not a man who walks the earth in a body of flesh and bones. Yet he is a personage of spirit who walks up and down the earth to tempt and destroy man. He is Lucifer who became Satan even the devil, and he is the father of all lies.

# THE SAGE

An adulterer is also a liar. He will lie to try and hide the truth but the truth will find him out in the end.

₤    ₤    ₤

Do not require God to have you understand the why of all things. Man is here to live by faith. If a man knew the answers to why, how, where and when the tests of life happen to him, he could not live by faith because he would already know all things

₤    ₤    ₤.

Faith is the first principle for under-standing all things. First one must believe. Then comes knowledge. Once a man knows a certain thing he no longer has to believe in that thing for he now knows it, yet if he continues to believe he will eventually find wisdom.

₤    ₤    ₤

What single practice has caused not only personal financial ruin but has also financially ruined entire nations? The answer is, the practice of usury. To charge excessive amounts of interest: when money is borrowed is not only criminal, it is evil. Be very wise when borrowing or lending money.

# THE SAGE

One can only keep that which one gives away. Every man has been given a gift from God. Find your gift and give it away. This is how to serve the sons and daughters of God. And when you give your gift to them and serve and minister to their needs, you will establish your own true identity and find peace in this life.

And now to all those who love God, I bid you adieu.

/

# About the Author

Ron Bartalini lives in Utah where he writes the lyrics and music to songs. He is the author of three picture books for children. Prince Galem and the Golden Key and Lollipop Molly are soon to be published. He has also written four books of poetry. This is his fifth inspirational book.